P9-CDI-422

HMH | into Reading™

my Book ❷

Authors and Advisors

Alma Flor Ada • Kylene Beers • F. Isabel Campoy
Joyce Armstrong Carroll • Nathan Clemens
Anne Cunningham • Martha C. Hougen
Elena Izquierdo • Carol Jago • Erik Palmer
Robert E. Probst • Shane Templeton • Julie Washington

Contributing Consultants

David Dockterman • Mindset Works®
Jill Eggleton

Copyright © 2020 by Houghton Mifflin Harcourt Publishing Company

All rights reserved. No part of this work may be reproduced or transmitted in any form or by any means, electronic or mechanical, including photocopying or recording, or by any information storage or retrieval system, without the prior written permission of the copyright owner unless such copying is expressly permitted by federal copyright law. Requests for permission to make copies of any part of the work should be submitted through our Permissions website at https://customercare.hmhco.com/contactus/Permissions. html or mailed to Houghton Mifflin Harcourt Publishing Company, Attn: Intellectual Property Licensing, 9400 Southpark Center Loop, Orlando, Florida 32819-8647.

Printed in the U.S.A.

ISBN   978-0-544-45880-2

4 5 6 7 8 9 10   2536   27 26 25 24 23 22 21 20 19

4500751448   B C D E F G

If you have received these materials as examination copies free of charge, Houghton Mifflin Harcourt Publishing Company retains title to the materials and they may not be resold. Resale of examination copies is strictly prohibited.

Possession of this publication in print format does not entitle users to convert this publication, or any portion of it, into electronic format.

my Book 2

MODULE 4

Better Together

🌐 **SOCIAL STUDIES CONNECTION:**

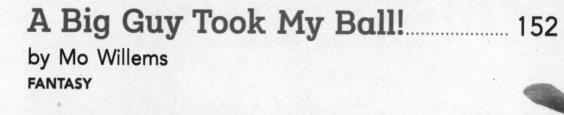

tap-tap-tap

my house

Amazing Animals

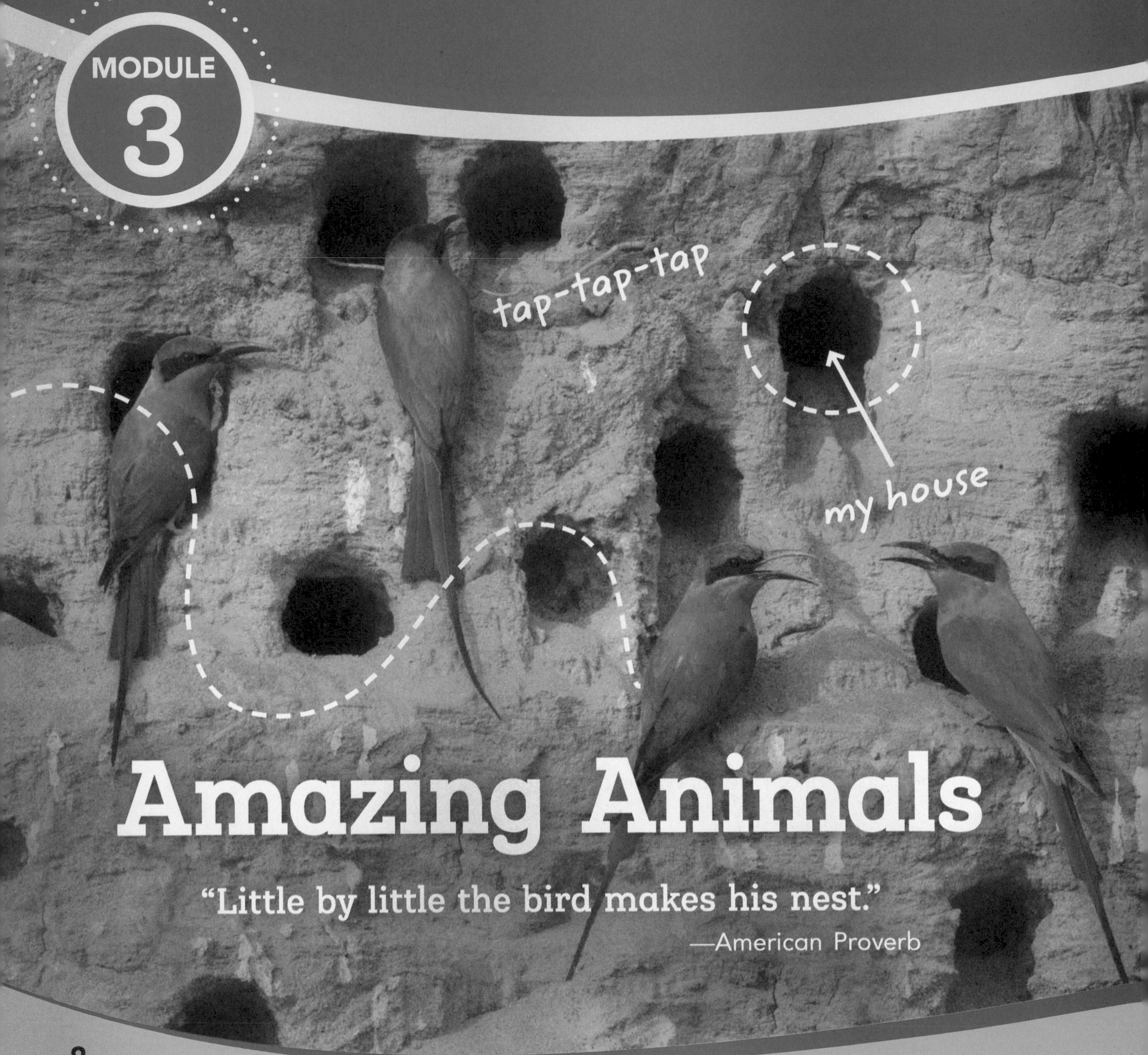

"Little by little the bird makes his nest."

—American Proverb

How do animals' bodies help them?

knock-knock

Words About How Animals Live

Complete the Vocabulary Network to show what you know about the words.

camouflage
Meaning: Camouflage is what hides something or makes it difficult to see.

Synonyms and Antonyms	Drawing

mammal

Meaning: A **mammal** is a kind of animal that has hair and feeds milk to its babies.

Synonyms and Antonyms	Drawing

characteristics

Meaning: **Characteristics** are things that make a person, animal, or thing different from others.

Synonyms and Antonyms	Drawing

Animal Q & A

Imagine that *you* had wings! What could *you* do? Find out what animals can do with *their* bodies!

Zip, zip, zip!

Knock! knock!

Q: What could you do with **wings?**

A: Swim! Penguins flap to go fast!

Q: What could you do with a **shell?**

A: Hide! Turtles are safe inside.

Whoosh!

Zzzzzzzz....

Q: What could you do with **trunk**?

A: Snorkel! Elephants get air like this.

Q: What could you do with **claws**?

A: Grab! Bats hang upside down to sleep.

Prepare to Read

GENRE STUDY **Realistic fiction** stories are made up but could happen in real life. Look for:

• characters and a setting that seem real

• ways the pictures and words work together to tell the story

SET A PURPOSE **Ask questions** before, during, and after you read to help you understand the text. Look for evidence in the text and pictures to **answer** your questions.

POWER WORDS
exclaimed
twigs
surprise
soon
warm
empty

Meet Nina de Polonia.

14

The Nest

by Carole Roberts

illustrated by
Nina de Polonia

"Max! Jen!" exclaimed Quin. "Look! I see a nest!"

"Can you see the nest?" asked Quin.

"I see it!" said Max and Jen.

"Can you see the bird?" asked Mrs. Web.

"Yes! It is a mockingbird," said Quin.

The nest was made of twigs.

It had grass in it.

"The grass will make it soft," said Ben.

"I see twigs and leaves," said Wes.

"I see bits of paper," said Liz.

"We can write about it!" said Jen.

One day, a surprise was in the nest.

"Eggs!" the kids said.
"We see eggs with dots!"

"We will look at the nest every day," said Mrs. Web.

"Will we see baby birds?" asked Quin. "Soon?" everyone asked.

The bird sat on the nest.
This made the eggs warm.

The bird sat and sat for days.

One day, the kids see baby birds!

The mom fed the baby birds.

The dad fed the baby birds.

"The baby birds look soft," said Liz.

"Soon they will get big feathers," said Quin.

Every day, the birds try to fly.

"Can they fly yet?" the kids asked.

The baby birds try.

Then the baby birds can fly!

One day, it was quiet.
The nest was empty.
It was fun to see the baby birds!

Turn and Talk

Use details from **The Nest** to answer these questions with a partner.

1. **Ask and Answer Questions** What questions did you ask yourself before, during, and after reading? How did they help you understand **The Nest**?

2. What important things happen after the bird lays the eggs?

Talking Tip

Be polite. Wait for your turn to tell your idea to your partner.

I think that _____.

Write a Journal Entry

PROMPT Think about what the birds did in **The Nest.** Write a journal entry to show what you learned.

PLAN First, draw a picture that shows an interesting fact you learned about birds or eggs.

WRITE Now write today's date. Write a sentence or two to explain the information your picture shows. Remember to:

- Begin the name of the month with a capital letter.

- Be sure each sentence tells a complete idea.

_____

- -

_____

- -

_____

- -

_____

- -

_____

- -

_____

Prepare to Read

GENRE STUDY **Realistic fiction** stories are made up but could happen in real life.

MAKE A PREDICTION Preview **The Pet Plan**. Think about events that could really happen in this realistic fiction story. What do you think it will be about?

_____

- -

_____

_____

- -

_____

SET A PURPOSE Ask yourself questions before, during, and after you read to help you understand what the kids do when something happens to the pet.

The Pet Plan

READ Describe an important event that happens in the beginning.

The kids had a pet at school.
They fed the pet every day.
But one day, the pet got out!
"Will we find our pet?" asked Jen.
"Yes!" said Ned. "I have a plan." ▶

Close Reading Tip

Number the main events in order.

CHECK MY UNDERSTANDING

Write a question you have about the story. Then read on to **see** if you can find the answer.

_____

- -

_____

- -

_____

"First, look in every place in the room," said Ned.

They did not find the pet.

"Then we will put out cookies," said Ned.

The kids sat and sat.

Zip! Zip! The pet ran out to get a cookie.

"Get the pet!" said Jim.

At last, the kids got the pet!

Then it was safe and warm in its nest.

CHECK MY UNDERSTANDING

Describe what happens to the pet at the end of the story.

_____

- -

_____

- -

_____

- -

_____

WRITE ABOUT IT What do you think happens next in the story? Add on to the story. Use words like **first, next, then,** and **last** to tell the events in order.

_____

- -

_____

- -

_____

- -

_____

- -

_____

- -

_____

- -

_____

- -

_____

Prepare to Read

GENRE STUDY **Folktales** are stories from long ago that have been told over and over. Look for:

- animals that act and talk like people
- storytelling phrases like **long ago**
- the reason an author tells a story

SET A PURPOSE Make pictures in your mind as you read. Words that tell how things look, sound, feel, taste, or smell and words about feelings can help you **create mental images**.

POWER WORDS

dull

thank

once

Meet James Bruchac.

Blue Bird and Coyote

a Native American tale, as told by James Bruchac

illustrated by Chris Lensch

Long ago, Blue Bird was not blue.
She was gray and dull.
How did she get her color?

One day, Gray Bird saw a lake.
It was beautiful!
A blue butterfly was at the lake.

"How did you get your color?"
asked Gray Bird.
"It is from the lake," said Butterfly.

"This is how to get it," said Butterfly.
"Go in the lake.
Do it four days in a row.
Then thank the lake."

43

Day 1

Day 2

Day 3

Day 4

Gray Bird did this.
Then she was blue!
"Thank you, lake!"

Long ago, Coyote was green.

Coyote saw Blue Bird.

"How did you get your color?" asked Coyote.

"I will tell you," said Blue Bird.

And she did.

Coyote went in the lake.
But, he did all four dips in one day!
Once he was blue, Coyote got out.
He did not thank the lake.

Coyote ran off to tell his friends.
But Coyote fell!
He went down,
        down,
                down a big hill.

Coyote got up.
Now he was all dusty and dull!

To this day, Blue Bird is blue.
And Coyote is dusty gray.

Use details from **Blue Bird and Coyote** to answer these questions with a partner.

1. Create Mental Images What pictures did you make in your mind when Blue Bird and Coyote got their colors? What words helped you create those pictures?

2. What do you think the author wants you to learn from the story?

Listening Tip

Listen carefully. Think about the meaning of what your partner is saying.

Write a Story Ending

PROMPT Coyote still wants blue fur! How will he get it? Make up an ending to add to **Blue Bird and Coyote**.

PLAN What is Coyote's new plan to get blue fur? Add three ideas to the chart.

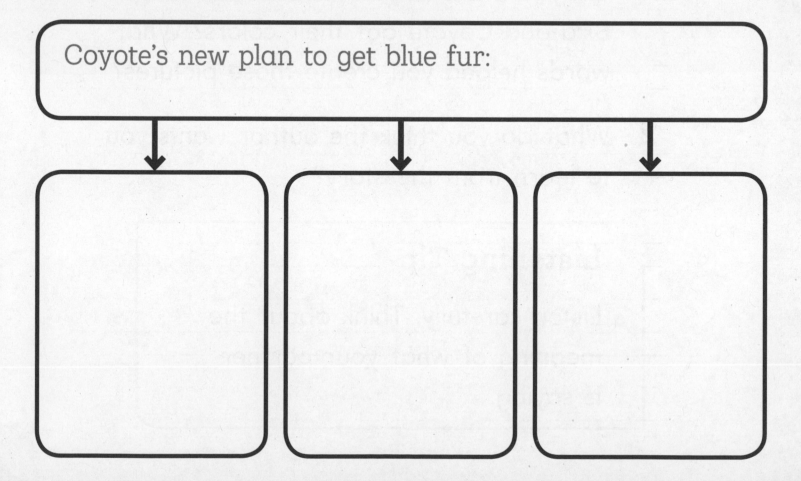

Coyote's new plan to get blue fur:

WRITE Now write what happens next in the story. Use another sheet of paper if you need to. Remember to:

- Tell how Coyote solves his problem.

- Be sure each sentence tells a complete idea.

_____

- - - - - - - - - - - - - - - - - - - -

_____

_____

- - - - - - - - - - - - - - - - - - - -

_____

_____

- - - - - - - - - - - - - - - - - - - -

_____

_____

- - - - - - - - - - - - - - - - - - - -

_____

_____

- - - - - - - - - - - - - - - - - - - -

_____

_____

- - - - - - - - - - - - - - - - - - - -

_____

Prepare to Read

GENRE STUDY **Folktales** are stories from long ago that have been told over and over.

MAKE A PREDICTION Preview **The Nut**. Blue Bird and Coyote are together again! This time they find a nut. What do you think will happen?

_____

_____

_____

_____

_____

_____

SET A PURPOSE Read to find out what Blue Bird and Coyote do with the nut. Find out if your prediction is right.

The Nut

READ <u>Underline</u> words that help you imagine what the nut is like.

One day, Blue Bird and Coyote find a
BIG green nut. Yum!
They tug, but the nut will not pop out!
Fox runs up and sees the big green nut.
Yum! Fox will help. ▶

Close Reading Tip
Write C when you
make a connection.

CHECK MY UNDERSTANDING

Picture in your mind what the nut is like. Why won't
it come out of the ground?

_____

- -

_____

- -

_____

READ Does one of the characters tell this story or is it a person not in the story? <u>Underline</u> words that tell you.

Close Reading Tip

Put a ! by a surprising part.

Cat and Dog help, too.

They all tug and tug and tug.

But the nut will not pop out!

Then Bug said that she will help.

"How can you help?" asked Fox.

"I have lots of little legs," she said.

They all tug together and . . .

POP! The big nut is out!

"Thank you, friends!" said Coyote.

CHECK MY UNDERSTANDING

What might the characters do with the nut? Why?

_____

- -

_____

_____

- -

_____

_____

- -

_____

WRITE ABOUT IT Think about what Coyote is like in **Blue Bird and Coyote** and **The Nut.** How are the things he does different in both stories? Why do you think he does different things?

_____

- -

_____

- -

_____

- -

_____

- -

_____

- -

_____

- -

_____

- -

_____

- -

_____

Prepare to Read

GENRE STUDY **Narrative nonfiction** gives information but sounds like a story. Look for:

- information about something real
- words that describe sounds and things
- a real setting

SET A PURPOSE As you read, stop and think if you don't understand something. Reread, look at the pictures, use what you already know, or ask yourself questions to help you figure it out.

POWER WORDS

stroll

shingle

shriek

Meet Kenard Pak.

HAVE YOU HEARD THE NESTING BIRD?

by Rita Gray   illustrated by Kenard Pak

Mourning doves take their morning stroll.

coah, cooo, cooo, coooo

Woodpecker calls from
a tree with a hole.

cuk-cuk-cuk-cuk-cuk

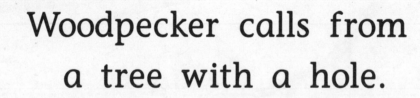

Starling sings from a metal pole.

whistle-ee-wee-tree

But have you heard the nesting bird?
"What bird? Where?"
"That robin, nesting up there."

Sparrow makes a simple jingle.

chiddik, chiddik

Swallow slides from under a shingle.

ha-ha-chit-chit-chit,
ha-ha-twitter-twit!

Crow calls out,
"Come meet and mingle!"
caw! caw! caw! caw!

But have you heard the nesting bird?
"Not a single tweet or trill."
"This nesting bird is so still!"

Cardinal wears a pointy hat.
cheer-cheer-cheer-
purdy-purdy-purdy

Chickadee is an acrobat.
chick-a-dee-dee-dee

Catbird sounds like a hungry cat.
meow! meow!

But have you heard
the nesting bird?
"It doesn't sing, not even a bit!"
"All it does is sit and sit."

Blue jay's shriek is
as sharp as a drill.
jay! jay!   jay! jay!

Whip-poor-will has
his favorite trill.
whip-poor-will   whip-poor-will

Wood thrush turns
the twilight still.
ee-oh-lay   ee-oh-laaay

But have you heard the nesting bird?
"It hasn't sung a single song."
"This bird has been sitting for so long!"

Wait, what's that . . . ?

Tapping   Cracking

"Something made a little sound!"

Breaking   Shaking

"The bird is starting to move around!"

Ruffling   Shuffling

"The bird flew off with something blue."

Cheeping   Peeping

"Look! Another robin is coming too!"

"The baby birds are here!"

HAVE YOU HEARD THE NESTING BIRD?
by Rita Gray illustrated by Kenard Pak

Turn and Talk

Use details from **Have You Heard the Nesting Bird?** to answer these questions with a partner.

1. **Monitor and Clarify** When you came to a part of the text you did not understand, what did you do to try to figure it out?

2. Why does the nesting bird sit so long?

Talking Tip

Ask a question if you are not sure about your partner's ideas.

Why did you say _____?

Write a Story

PROMPT Imagine that you are with the kids in **Have You Heard the Nesting Bird?** What do you see the nesting bird do?

PLAN Draw pictures to show the main things the nesting bird does **first, next,** and **last.**

First	Next	Last

WRITE Now write your own version of the story. Tell what you saw the nesting bird do. Use another sheet of paper if you need it. Remember to:

- Use **first, next,** and **last** to show the order of events.

- Use words to describe the nesting bird.

Prepare to Read

GENRE STUDY **Narrative nonfiction** gives information but sounds like a story.

MAKE A PREDICTION Preview **Bird News**. A student author wrote a newspaper story about real birds. What do you think you will learn?

_____

- -

_____

_____

- -

_____

_____

- -

_____

SET A PURPOSE Read to find out which birds the student saw and what they are like. If a part is not clear, reread, look at the pictures, use what you know, or ask yourself questions to figure it out.

Crow

Bird News

READ **READ** What is the author describing in this part?

This is my bird news!

I saw a crow in my neighborhood.

Like all birds, crows have many feathers and a beak.

This crow had a nest made of twigs.

It had four dull-blue eggs in its nest.

Close Reading Tip

<u>Underline</u> the important describing words.

CHECK MY UNDERSTANDING

Describe the crow. Use details from the text and photo.

_____

- - - - - - - - - - - - - - - - - - - -

_____

_____

- - - - - - - - - - - - - - - - - - - -

_____

READ <u>Underline</u> what the author is describing in this part. The author describes two birds in two different parts. How does this help you understand the text?

Close Reading Tip

Mark important ideas with *.

I saw a mom robin, too.

It sat on a nest made of little twigs.

The mom robin got up from the nest.

I saw beautiful blue eggs in it!

Then I saw the robin fly back to the nest.

I will write news about the baby birds once they are out of the eggs!

CHECK MY UNDERSTANDING

When you came to a part you did not understand, what did you do to try to figure it out?

_____

- -

_____

- -

_____

- -

_____

DRAW IT Draw a robin or a crow and its nest. Use information from **Bird News** to color and label your picture. Then share facts about the bird with a partner. Show your picture to help you describe it.

Prepare to Read

GENRE STUDY **Procedural texts** tell how to do or make something. Look for:

- directions to follow
- numbered steps that are in order
- pictures that help you understand

SET A PURPOSE Read to understand the most important ideas. Look for details in the words and pictures to help you. **Summarize** by telling the important ideas in your own words.

POWER WORDS
predators
prey
school
circling
herd

Meet Steve Jenkins and Robin Page.

Step-by-Step Advice from the Animal Kingdom

by Steve Jenkins & Robin Page

from **How to Swallow a Pig**

How to
Defend
Yourself
Like an Armadillo

❶ Freeze!

Many predators don't notice prey unless it's moving. Holding still can be a good tactic.

❷ Run.

Armadillos can move quickly. So can you. If freezing doesn't work, don't just sit there.

❸ Dig.

Start digging a hole. Use your long claws. Work quickly! You'll soon have a burrow to hide in.

4 Swim.

You're a good swimmer. And not every predator likes to get wet.

5 Leap.

Try jumping a few feet up into the air. This can startle even the fiercest predator. It can give you time to escape.

6 Hunker down.

If all else fails, pull in your head and feet. And hope your armor persuades the attacker to give up.

How to
Spin a Web
Like a Spider

1 **Cast a line.**

Cast a single silk thread into the air. If you're lucky, the breeze will catch it. It will snag on a nearby branch or other object.

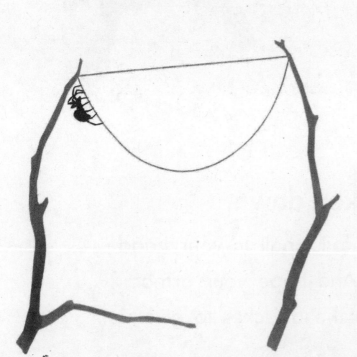

2 **Make a loop.**

Walk across the first thread. Spin another that droops to form a U.

3 Turn your U into a Y.

Drop a line from the bottom
of the loose thread. Tighten
it to make a Y shape.

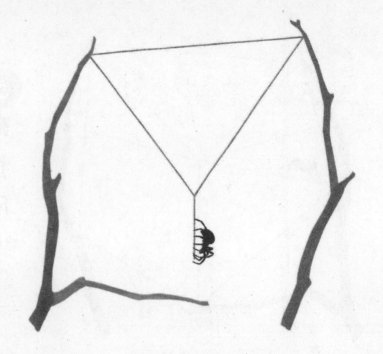

4 Frame your web.

Spin threads that will form
the borders of your web.

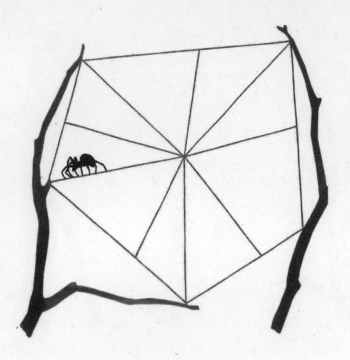

5 Spin threads from the center to the edges.

These lines form the framework for your web. They give you unsticky threads to walk on.

6 Make a spiral.

Make a spiral of silk. So far, none of the threads you've spun are sticky.

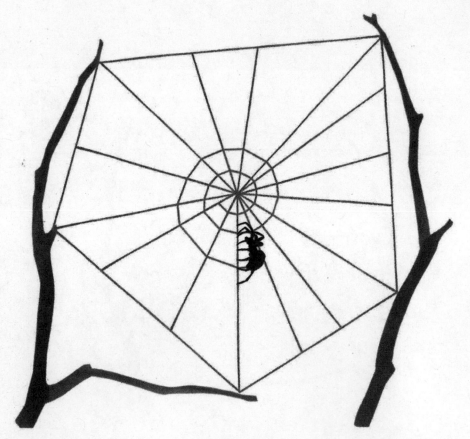

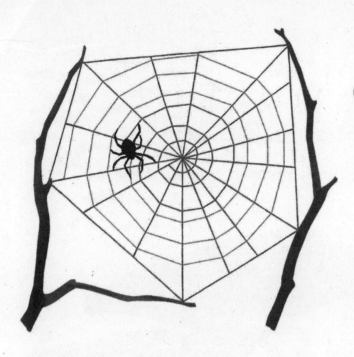

7 Get sticky.

Now work your way back to the center. Lay down sticky threads. The original spiral will be your path. You'll recycle it by eating it as you go.

8 Wait for dinner.

Now you can rest. Sit in the center of your new web. Wait for an insect to blunder into your trap.

How to
Trap Fish
Like a Humpback Whale

1 **Find some fish.**

The first step is locating a school of fish. Some of these schools include millions of fish.

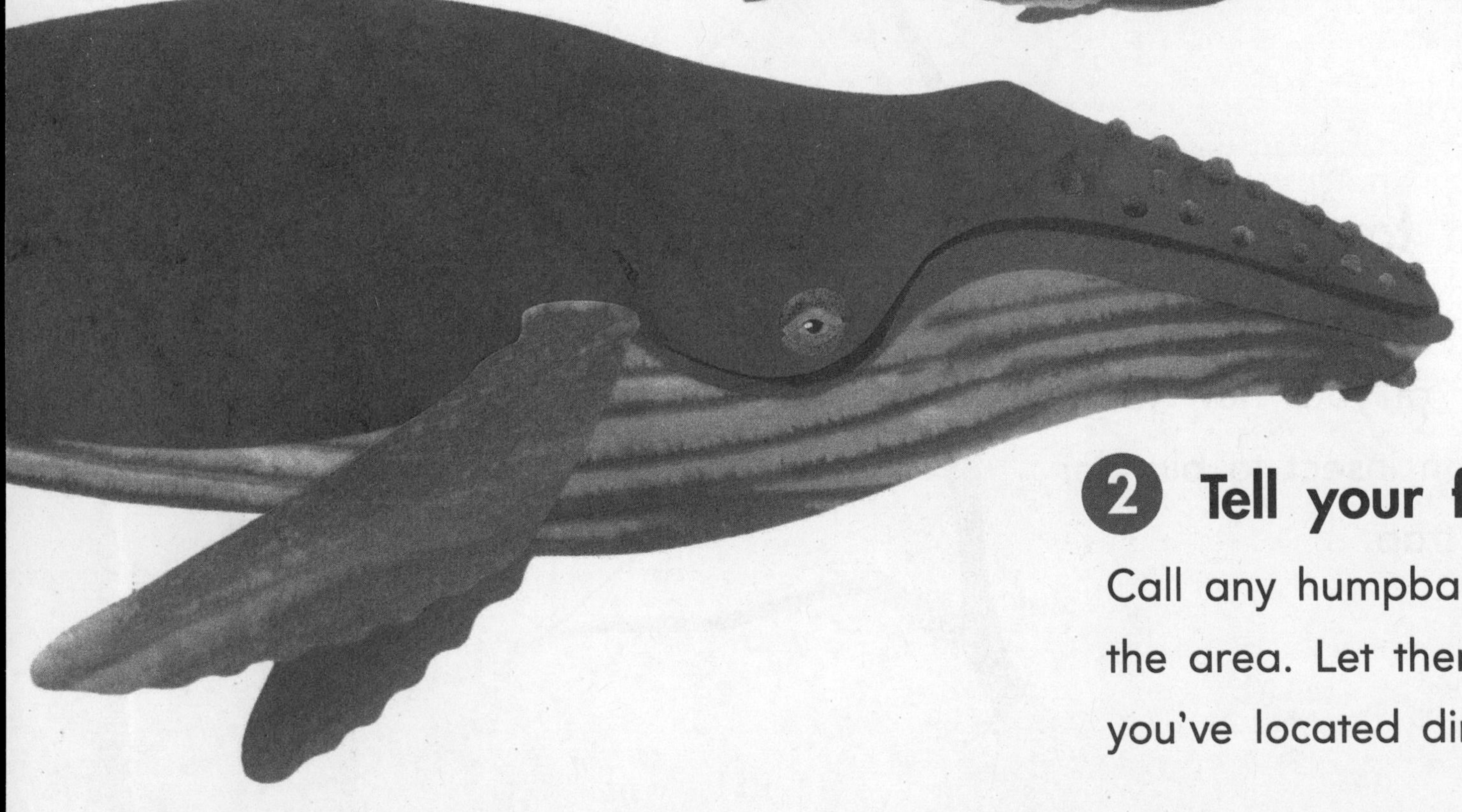

2 **Tell your friends.**

Call any humpbacks in the area. Let them know you've located dinner.

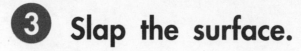

③ Slap the surface.

Whacking the water with your tail frightens the fish. It makes them swim closer together. If you don't have a tail, ask one of the whales for help.

④ Swim in circles.

Join the whales in circling beneath the fish. Blow bubbles. Herd the fish together by swimming in smaller and smaller circles.

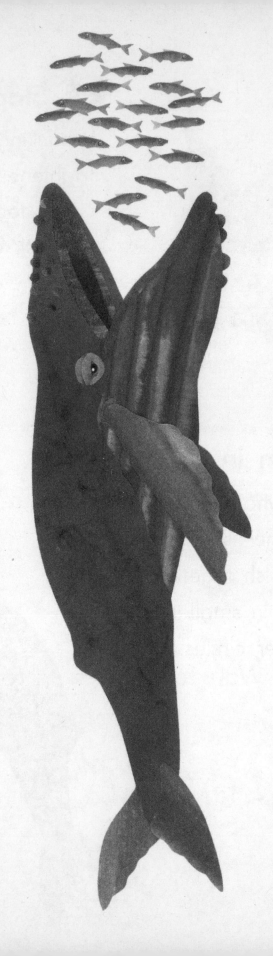

5 Gulp!

Take turns swimming up.
Open your mouth wide.
Swallow as many fish as
you can in one gulp.

Use details from **Step-by-Step Advice from the Animal Kingdom** to answer these questions with a partner.

1. **Summarize** What are the most important ideas this text is about?

2. Which animal's body helps it the best? Use ideas from the text to tell why.

Talking Tip

Wait for your turn to talk. Explain your ideas and feelings clearly.

I feel that _____.

Write a Fact

PROMPT You learned a lot about animals in **Step-by-Step Advice from the Animal Kingdom**. What was the most interesting fact?

PLAN First, draw a picture of the animal and write words to tell about the most interesting fact.

WRITE Now write your fact. Use your picture and notes for ideas. Remember to:

- Tell true information.

- Be sure your sentence tells a complete idea.

_____

_____

_____

_____

_____

_____

_____

_____

_____

_____

_____

Prepare to Read

GENRE STUDY **Procedural texts** tell how to do or make something.

MAKE A PREDICTION Preview **Pop-Up Armadillo**. Look at the features, like the numbers and pictures. What do you think you will learn?

_____

- -

_____

_____

- -

_____

_____

- -

_____

SET A PURPOSE Read to find out how to make a pop-up armadillo. Find clues that the text is organized to explain the steps in order.

Pop-Up Armadillo

READ <u>Underline</u> words and other things that show the order of the steps.

You can make a pop-up armadillo!

1. First, get what you see in **1** at the top.

2. Then color an armadillo.

   Do not make it too big.

   Do not make it too little.

   Make it fit.

> ### Close Reading Tip
> Mark important ideas with *.

CHECK MY UNDERSTANDING

What is the most important idea in this part?

_____

- - - - - - - - - - - - - - - - - - - -

_____

- - - - - - - - - - - - - - - - - - - -

_____

5

READ What are the most important ideas in this part? Tell why you think the author wrote **Pop-Up Armadillo**.

Close Reading Tip

Circle words you don't know. Then figure them out.

3 Cut out the armadillo.

Do not cut the border!

Look at **3** on page 97 to see how.

4 Then bend back the top border.

Color all of it to make it look great!

5 Last, cut up paper to make grass.

Add it to the pop-up.

Now tell your classmates about your armadillo!

CHECK MY UNDERSTANDING

Why did the author write the steps in order?

_____

- -

_____

- -

_____

- -

_____

WRITE ABOUT IT In your own words, write the most important ideas you learned about making a pop-up animal. Use words like **first, next, then,** and **last** to help you tell things in order.

_____

- -

_____

_____

- -

_____

_____

- -

_____

_____

- -

_____

_____

- -

_____

_____

- -

_____

Prepare to View

GENRE STUDY **Videos** are short movies. Some videos give information. Others are for you to watch for enjoyment. Watch and listen for:

- information about the topic
- how the pictures and words work together

SET A PURPOSE Find out about beavers! Notice what the beavers do and how the events are shown in the order that they happen during the year. Think about how having the events in order helps you understand the video.

Build Background: Beaver Dams

Beaver Family

from National Geographic Kids

As You View Notice how the video has a beginning, middle, and end. The events happen in order. How does this help you understand the video? Use the words and pictures to find out what the beavers do before, during, and after winter.

Beaver Family

Turn and Talk

Use details from **Beaver Family** to answer these questions with a partner.

1. **Chronological Order** What important things do beavers do before winter? What do they do during winter? Then what do they do in the spring?

2. How does a beaver use its body to build a dam?

Listening Tip

Listen carefully. Make connections. How is what your partner says like other things you know?

Let's Wrap Up!

? Essential Question

How do animals' bodies help them?

··

Pick one of these activities to show what you have learned about the topic.

1. **Animal <u>Do</u>s and <u>Don't</u>s**

Pick an animal you have read about. Talk to a partner. Describe what the animal should do and should not do to survive. Complete these sentences:

Do _____.

Don't _____.

104

2. Animal Babies

Draw a picture of one of the animals you read about. Write to explain how the mom or dad animal would take care of the babies. Share your writing with classmates.

Word Challenge

Can you use characteristics to help you explain?

My Notes

Better Together

"What you do not want done to
yourself, do not do to others."

—Confucius

Why is it important to do my best and get along with others?

Get Curious
Video

Words About Being Good Citizens

Complete the Vocabulary Network to show what you know about the words.

honest

Meaning: If you are an **honest** person, you tell the truth.

Synonyms and Antonyms	Drawing

sport

Meaning: A good **sport** plays fair and gets along with others.

Synonyms and Antonyms	Drawing

courtesy

Meaning: If you do something as a **courtesy**, you do it to be kind or polite.

Synonyms and Antonyms	Drawing

GOOD SPORTS

★ Is it good to be a good sport?
Find out one person's opinion. ★

I think it's important to be a good sport. Here's why! Good sports play fair. They follow the rules. Everyone has more fun when a game is fair. Also, good sports are good teammates. They take turns. They try hard and work together to score points. They cheer for others.

We did it!
Your turn!

Finally, good sports are nice to be with. They don't get grouchy about who wins or loses. They think it's fun just to play! So, be a good sport. You will have fun, and others will, too!

Prepare to Read

GENRE STUDY ▶ **Informational text** is nonfiction. It gives facts about a topic or real people. Look for:

- photographs of a real person
- facts about real events
- pictures with labels

SET A PURPOSE ▶ Think about the author's words as you read. Then decide, or **evaluate**, which details are the most important to help you understand the text.

POWER WORDS

team

equipment

coach

rules

goal

fan

Meet Jane Medina.

GOAL!

by Jane Medina
illustrated by Maine Diaz

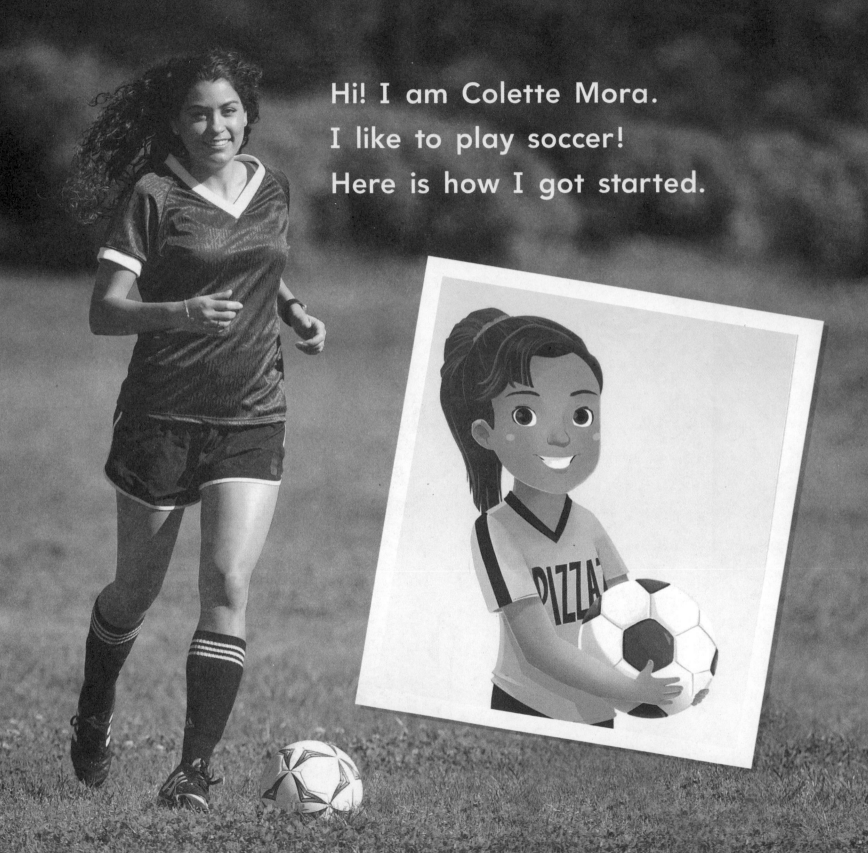

Hi! I am Colette Mora.
I like to play soccer!
Here is how I got started.

Today I get to be on my very first soccer team!
I see my twin Yvonne and my friend Brittney.

smile

ball

sock

shin guard

cleats

We have our equipment.
We will have such fun!

Mr. Chan will coach us.

"Pick a number for your uniform," he tells us.

Yvonne picks six.

Brittney picks ten.

I pick 12.

I am at my first practice.
Coach tells us the rules.
"Kick the ball.
Do not use your hands.
But the goalie *can* use her
hands to get the ball."

118

"The rules help you play fair and be safe. Then we can *all* have fun!"

Coach tells us how to pass the ball.
I kick it, and Brittney kicks it back.
Coach tells us how to dribble the ball.
"Kick it a little.
Then run to it," he tells us.

Kick, run, kick, run, kick, run.
Little by little, we find out how
to play soccer.

I am at my first game.
The referee tells us to play fair.
Then we play!

I pass the ball to Brittney.

She kicks it to Yvonne.

Kick, pass, kick, pass.

Yvonne kicks it back to me.
I dribble the ball.
"Run, Colette!" Coach yells.
I am very quick!

The goalie runs to get the ball.

I kick it at the net. Then . . .

GOAL!

I got my very first goal!

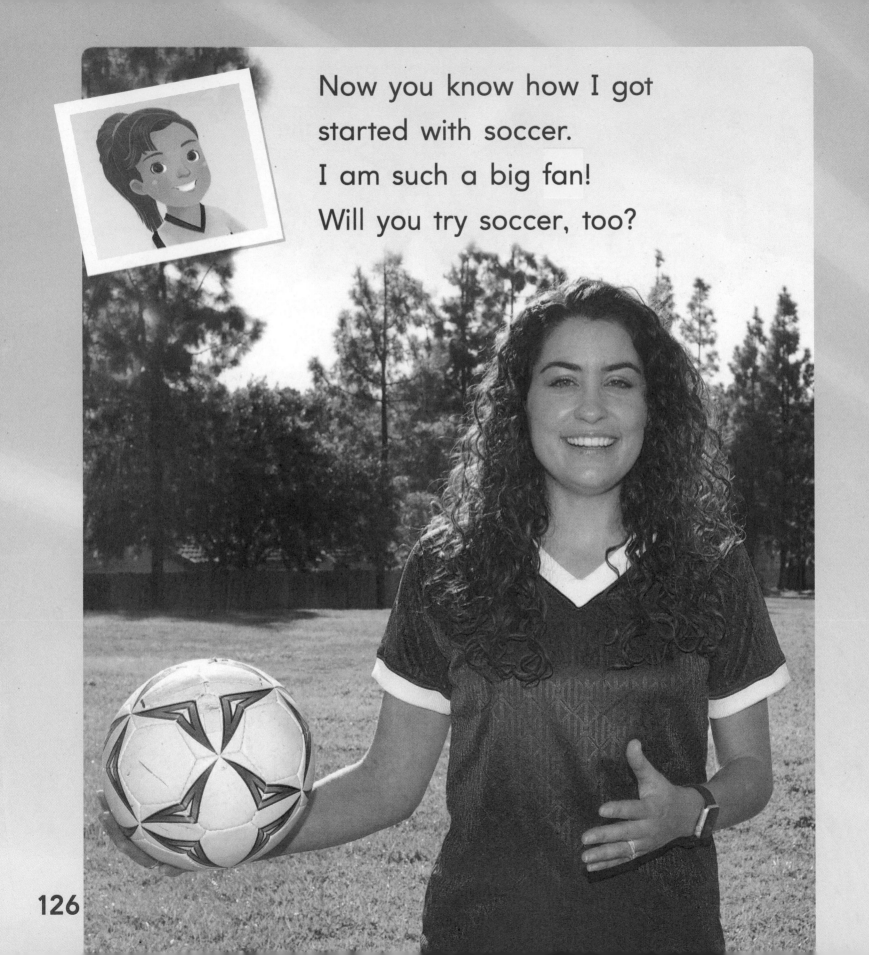

Now you know how I got
started with soccer.
I am such a big fan!
Will you try soccer, too?

126

Turn and Talk

GOAL!

by Jane Medina
Illustrated by Maine Diaz

Use details from **Goal!** to answer these questions with a partner.

1. **Evaluate** Which details in **Goal!** are the most important for helping you understand why Colette likes soccer?

2. How do Colette and her team feel when she gets a goal? Why?

Talking Tip

Wait for your turn to talk. Explain your ideas and feelings clearly.

I think that _____.

READ
Together

Write Game Rules

PROMPT How do you play soccer? Use details from the words and pictures in **Goal!** to explain the rules you learned.

PLAN First, write important words from **Goal!** that tell about playing soccer.

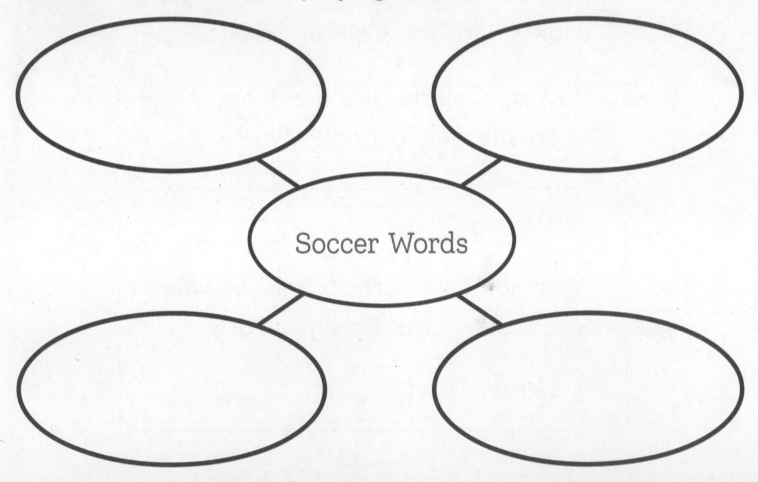

Soccer Words

WRITE Now write the rules for playing soccer in your own words. Remember to:

- Use soccer words from your web.

- Use verbs to tell about actions.

_____

_____

_____

_____

_____

_____

_____

_____

_____

_____

_____

Prepare to Read

GENRE STUDY **Informational text** is nonfiction. It gives facts about a topic.

MAKE A PREDICTION Preview **Chess Fan**. A boy finds out that his school has a chess team. What do you think he will do?

_____

_____

_____

_____

_____

_____

SET A PURPOSE Read to find out if the boy joins the chess team.

Chess Fan

READ What is an important reason to want to play chess?

I am Max. My school has a chess team. Chess looks like a lot of fun. I want to try it! This is how I started to play chess.

Coach sets up the chess game. She tells us all the rules. Meg is my first partner. ▶

Close Reading Tip

Put a ? by the parts you have questions about.

CHECK MY UNDERSTANDING

Who is telling this story? How do you know?

_____

- - - - - - - - - - - - - - - - - - -

_____

- - - - - - - - - - - - - - - - - - -

_____

READ What are the most important ideas to remember about playing chess? <u>Underline</u> them.

Close Reading Tip

Write C when you make a connection.

Then we practice. You have to practice to play well. Meg and I play lots of games of chess. Meg is a good partner, and I am, too. We play by the rules. We play fair.

Now I play on the chess team. I play chess every day. I am such a big chess fan!

CHECK MY UNDERSTANDING

The children are good partners because

_____

- -

_____

- -

_____

- -

_____

WRITE ABOUT IT What do you need to do to be a good chess player? Write facts you learned from **Chess Fan**. Then share your writing with a partner.

_____

- -

_____

- -

_____

- -

_____

- -

_____

- -

_____

- -

_____

- -

_____

- -

_____

- -

_____

Prepare to Read

GENRE STUDY **Informational text** is nonfiction. It gives facts about a topic. Look for:

- headings that stand out

- photographs

- a chart that shows information

SET A PURPOSE Read to find out the most important ideas in each part. Then **synthesize**, or put the ideas together in your mind, to find out new things about the text and what it really means to you.

POWER WORDS
well
exercise
body

Meet Rozanne Lanczak Williams.

134

Get UP and GO!

by Rozanne Lanczak Williams

Why Exercise?

When you are healthy, you are well.

You can get healthy and fit.

How? Exercise!

Get up and go!
This is the way.
Exercise
an hour a day!

Exercise Every Day

How can you get exercise?
You could walk.
Walk as much as you can!

A walk is great!
It is fun to skate!

Exercise with Friends

You could swim and hike with friends.
Many kids like bikes.

Play a Game

You could play hopscotch.

You could play fetch with your dog.

Jump and hop.
Play games with Pop.

Get Set . . .

It is good to stretch your **body**. This is a great way to warm up your muscles.

Stretch like a cat, this way and that!

Go!

Then you could go for a run.
Just run for fun!
Play tag with your friends.

Jog up a hill.
Then run down.
Jog back,
and jog to town.

Be on a Team

You can find out how to pitch and catch.
You can kick, toss, and pass a ball!

Be a Good Sport

Good sports try.

Good sports play fair.

Good sports have fun when they win and when they do not.

Do you know why it is fun to try?

It Is Up to You!

How will you get exercise?
Just get up and go!

If You Like to . . .   **You Can Try . . .**

run

jump

kick

Turn and Talk

Use details from **Get Up and Go!** to answer these questions with a partner.

1. **Synthesize** What is exercise? Why is exercise important for you?

2. What kinds of exercise can you do on your own? What kinds can you do with others?

Listening Tip

Listen carefully. Think of questions you want to ask your partner when it is your turn to talk.

Write an Opinion

PROMPT Which way of exercising from **Get Up and Go!** do you think is the best? Use details from the text to help you explain why.

PLAN First, write the kind of exercise you think is best. Write notes about your reasons why.

Reason

Reason

Reason

The best exercise is _____.

WRITE Now write sentences to tell which way of exercising you think is best. Tell reasons why. Remember to:

- Tell your opinion.

- Use the word **because** when you write a reason.

Prepare to Read

GENRE STUDY **Informational text** is nonfiction. It gives facts about a topic.

MAKE A PREDICTION Preview **Play Tag!** Use the title, headings, pictures, and chart to help you predict. What do you think you will learn?

_____

- -

_____

- -

_____

- -

_____

SET A PURPOSE Read to find out how and why to play tag.

Play Tag!

READ Why is the title big? Why are some words red? What do the red words tell you about this part?

Rules for Tag

Tag is a fun game that friends can play together. Pick one friend to be It. Then everyone runs. The friend who is It runs, too. If the friend who is It can catch you, then you are the new It!

> **Close Reading Tip**
> Write C when you make a connection.

CHECK MY UNDERSTANDING

Why is the player who is It important in tag?

_____

- - - - - - - - - - - - - - - - - - -

_____

- - - - - - - - - - - - - - - - - - -

_____

READ What are the two parts of the chart? What do you learn about tag from each part?

How Tag Helps You

Do you know how to be healthy? Play tag!

💡 **Close Reading Tip**

Mark important words with *.

Helps Your Body	Helps You Be Happy
It is good exercise.	Tag is fun.
You run a lot.	A fun game makes you happy.
It is good for your muscles.	Many friends can play together.

CHECK MY UNDERSTANDING

What important things did you learn about tag?

_____

_____

_____

_____

_____

WRITE ABOUT IT After reading **Play Tag!**, how
do you feel about the game? Write sentences to tell
what playing tag means to you. Use ideas from
Play Tag! to give reasons for why you think as you
do. Share your writing with classmates.

_____

_____

_____

_____

_____

Prepare to Read

GENRE STUDY **Fantasy** stories have made-up events that could not really happen. Look for:

- animals that talk and act like people
- ways the pictures help you understand
- a problem and resolution

SET A PURPOSE Read to understand events in the beginning, middle, and end. Look for details in the words and pictures to help you. **Retell** the events in your own words.

POWER WORDS

guy

hero

excuse

Meet Mo Willems.

A Big Guy Took My Ball!

by Mo Willems

Gerald!

I found a big ball,

and it was *so* fun!

HE TOOK

MY BALL!

159

He is so BIGGY-BIG- BIG- Gerald.

You did not get my big ball back, did you.

. . .

I did not.

EXCUSE

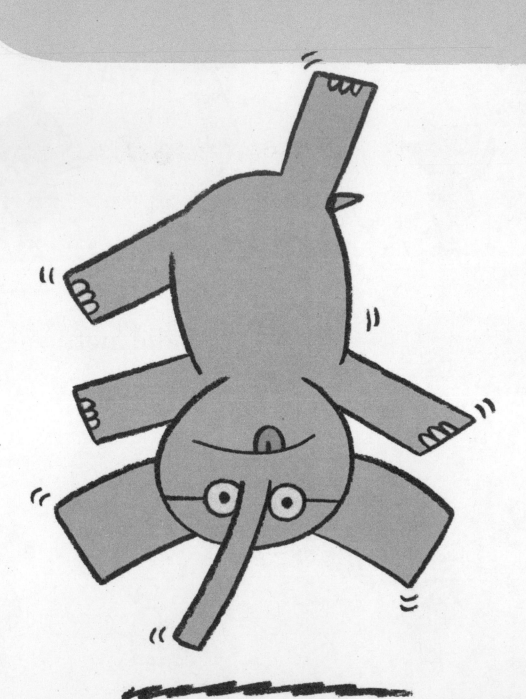

ME!

174

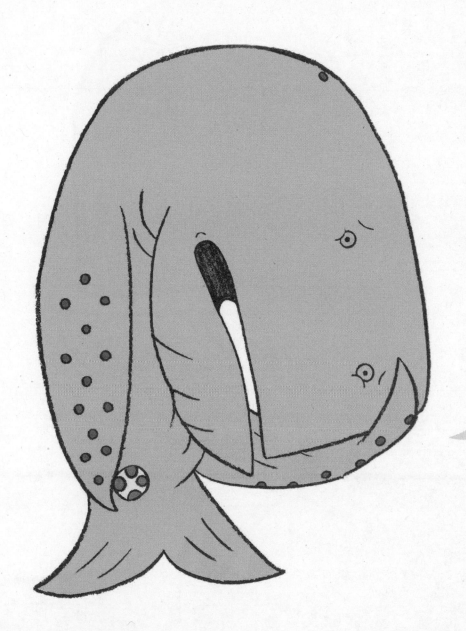

SO BIG THAT NO ONE WILL PLAY WITH ME.

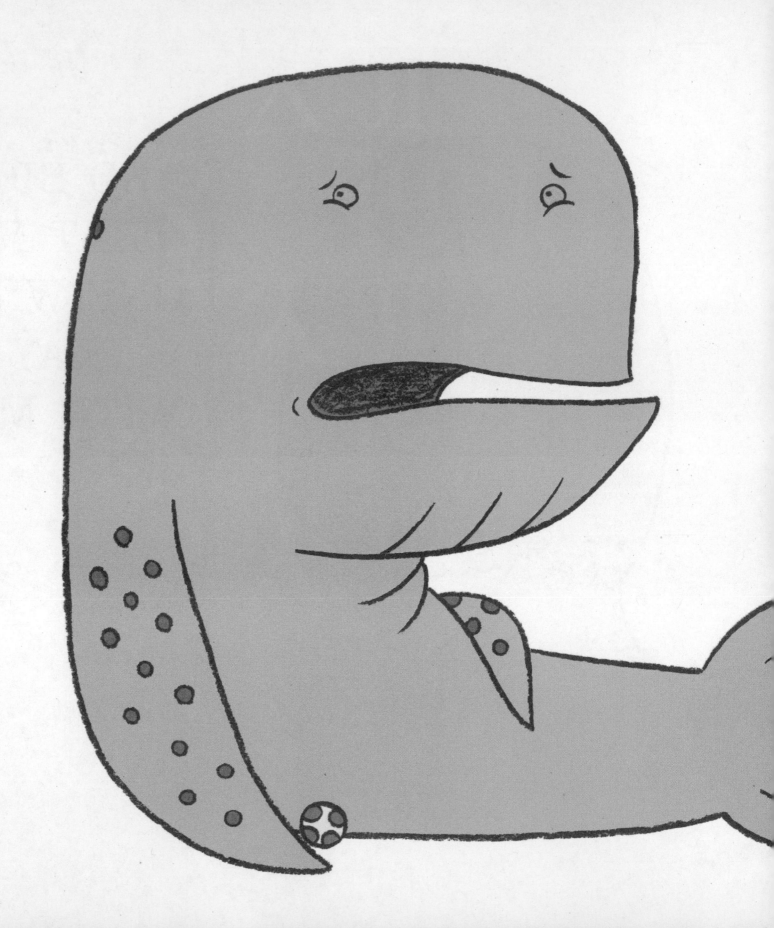

LITTLE GUYS HAVE
ALL THE FUN.

181

Turn and Talk

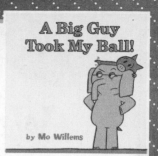

A Big Guy
Took My Ball!

by Mo Willems

Use details from **A Big Guy Took My Ball!** to answer these questions with a partner.

1. **Retell** Tell the story in your own words. Tell about the main events that happen in the beginning, middle, and end.

2. How do Gerald's ideas about big guys change during the story?

Talking Tip

Speak clearly. Do not speak too fast or too slow.

My idea is _____.

Write Game Directions

PROMPT How will the characters in **A Big Guy Took My Ball!** play "Whale Ball"? Write directions for the game. Use the story for ideas.

PLAN First, write or draw what to do to play "Whale Ball." Add numbers to show the order of the steps.

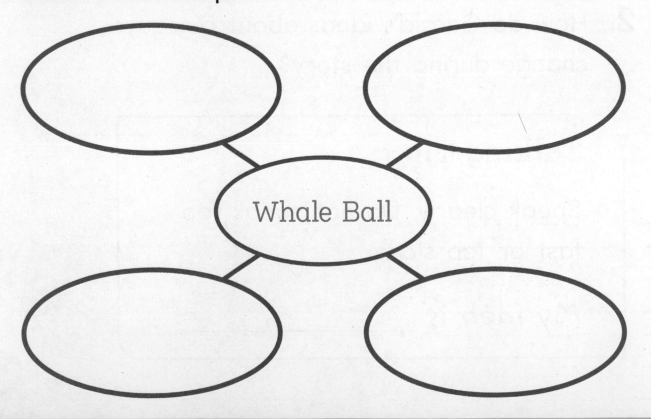

Whale Ball

WRITE Now write the directions for how to play "Whale Ball." Remember to:

- Write the steps in order.
- Use verbs to tell about actions.

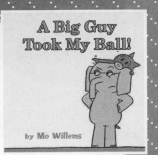

Prepare to Read

GENRE STUDY **Fantasy** stories have made-up events that could not really happen.

MAKE A PREDICTION Preview **Biggy-Big-Big!** Fox is always bragging about how big he is. What do you think will happen?

_____

- -

_____

_____

- -

_____

_____

- -

_____

SET A PURPOSE Read to find out what Fox does and what happens. Find out if your prediction is right.

Biggy-Big-Big!

READ <u>Underline</u> the names of the characters. Describe them.

"Look at me!" said Fox. "See how great I am? I am bigger than you, Duck. I am bigger than you, Bug. I am bigger than everyone. I am biggy-big-big!" Fox would not play with Duck and Bug. It made them sad. ▶

Close Reading Tip

Number the main events in order.

CHECK MY UNDERSTANDING

Why do you think Fox acts the way he does?

_____

- -

_____

- -

_____

READ What is Baby Yak like? <u>Underline</u> words that tell.

<u>Close Reading Tip</u>

Put a ? by the parts you have questions about.

Just then, Baby Yak ran by. She saw Duck and Bug. "Will you play with me?" Baby Yak asked them in a kind way.

Duck said, "Look, Fox! Baby Yak will play with us. And she is much bigger than you."

Fox saw that Baby Yak was BIGGY-BIG-BIG! He said, "I am very sorry, Duck and Bug."

CHECK MY UNDERSTANDING

How does Fox change by the end of the story?

_____

_____

_____

_____

DRAW IT Draw a picture of what you think the animals do after Fox says he is sorry. Add a caption to tell about it. Then tell the whole story **Biggy-Big-Big!** to a partner. Tell the main events that happen in the beginning, middle, and end.

_____

- -

_____

- -

_____

Prepare to Read

GENRE STUDY **Fantasy** stories have made-up events that could not really happen. Look for:

- animals that act like people
- a lesson the characters learn
- ways pictures help you understand

SET A PURPOSE As you read, **make connections** by finding ways that this text is like things in your life and other texts you have read. This will help you understand and remember the text.

POWER WORDS
seed
short
heap
trouble
fruits

Meet Kadir Nelson.

If You Plant a Seed

by Kadir Nelson

If you plant a tomato seed,

a carrot seed,

and a cabbage seed,

in time,

with love and care,

193

tomato,
carrot,
and cabbage
plants will grow.

If you plant a seed

of selfishness,

in a very short time,

it will grow,

and grow,

and grow

into a heap

of trouble.

But if you plant
a seed of kindness,

203

in almost no time at all,

the fruits of kindness

205

will

grow,

and

grow,

206

and

grow,

207

and they are very, very sweet.

208

Turn and Talk

Use details from **If You Plant a Seed** to answer these questions with a partner.

1. Make Connections Think about what happens to all the friends in this story. How is this like what happens to the friends in **A Big Guy Took My Ball**?

2. What do the characters do to be kind?

Listening Tip

Listen carefully. Look at your partner to show that you are paying attention.

Write a Book Report

PROMPT What lesson did you learn from **If You Plant a Seed**? Write a book report to tell others about the story and how you feel about it.

PLAN First, write about the lesson you learned. Write what you like and do not like about the story.

Lesson	I Like	I Do Not Like

WRITE Now write your book report. First, tell the title. Tell about the lesson you learned. Then tell what you like or do not like. Use another sheet of paper if you need it. Remember to:

• Use the story for ideas.

• Give reasons for your opinions.

Prepare to Read

GENRE STUDY **Fantasy** stories have made-up events that could not really happen.

MAKE A PREDICTION Preview **Fox and Crow**. Fox and Crow invite each other over for a meal. What do you think will happen?

_____

- -

_____

_____

- -

_____

_____

- -

_____

SET A PURPOSE Read to find out what happens when Fox and Crow eat together. Find out if your prediction is right.

Fox and Crow

READ What does Crow do that Fox does not like? <u>Underline</u> it.

One day, I asked Fox to eat a snack with me. Fox said "Yes!" My plan was to have a little fun with Fox. When he got to my nest, I set out seeds to eat. Just seeds. Fox was quiet. Then he said, "Crow, I am not a bird! I don't eat seeds! I am out of here!" ▶

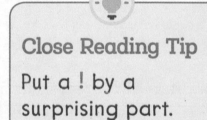

Close Reading Tip

Put a ! by a surprising part.

CHECK MY UNDERSTANDING

When have you felt like Fox feels?

_____

- - - - - - - - - - - - - - - - - - -

_____

- - - - - - - - - - - - - - - - - - -

_____

READ Who tells this part of the story? How do you know?

Crow made me mad, but she is still my friend. I asked her to eat with me. Soon Crow got to my den. I set out seeds for her to eat. I set out cookies for me.

"Fox, you have seeds for me!" Crow said. "How kind of you! Thank you. You are such a good friend! I am sorry that I was not kind to you before."

CHECK MY UNDERSTANDING

What lesson about kindness do you learn from this story?

_____

- -

_____

_____

- -

_____

- -

_____

Cite Text Evidence

WRITE ABOUT IT How are the things that happen in **Fox and Crow** like what happens in **If You Plant a Seed**? Write to explain. Use ideas from both stories.

Prepare to View

GENRE STUDY **Videos** are short movies. Some videos give information. Others are for you to watch for enjoyment. Watch and listen for:

• how pictures and sounds work together

• how the video makes you feel

• a lesson you can learn

SET A PURPOSE Watch the video to find out what **central idea**, or important message, it shares. Look for details that help you understand it.

Build Background: Kindness

COLOR

Your World with Kindness

from BetterWorldians Foundation

As You View Notice when the pictures change from gray to color. What happens each time one person helps another? Use details like these to figure out what the main message of the video is. How would you say this central idea in your own words?

READ Together

Use details from **Color Your World with Kindness** to answer these questions with a partner.

1. **Central Idea** What is the central idea you learn about kindness? Use details from the video to explain.

2. Describe the ways the people in the video help each other.

Talking Tip

Add on to what your partner says.

My idea is _____.

Let's Wrap Up!

? Essential Question

Why is it important to do my best and get along with others?

Pick one of these activities to show what you have learned about the topic.

1. **Character Remix**

Pick two characters from two different texts you read. Imagine that they meet. Draw a picture of them working together or being kind to each other. Write about your picture.

2. Dear Good Citizen

Write a letter to the character you read about who you think is the best citizen. Give reasons why he or she is the best. Read your letter to a partner. Talk about it.

Word Challenge

Can you use the word courtesy to help explain one of your reasons?

My Notes

Glossary

B

body

body Your **body** is made up of all your parts, like your head, arms, and legs.
You move your whole **body** when you dance.

C

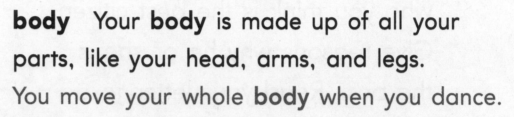

camouflage

camouflage Camouflage is what hides something or makes it difficult to see.
The animal's tan fur and spots are its **camouflage** in the grass.

characteristics Characteristics are things that make a person, animal, or thing different from others.
Short tails and long ears are **characteristics** of rabbits.

circling   If you are **circling** something, you keep moving around it in a circle.
A bird was **circling** its nest before it landed in it.

coach   If you **coach** people, you tell and show them how to do something.
My dad likes to **coach** my soccer team.

courtesy   If you do something as a **courtesy**, you do it to be kind or polite.
He had the **courtesy** to help his grandma when it was raining.

courtesy

D

dull   When something is **dull**, it is not bright.
It was a cloudy, **dull** day.

dull

223

E

empty

equipment

empty   If something is **empty**, it does not have anything in it.
I ate all my food, and now my bowl is **empty**.

equipment   Your **equipment** is the stuff you need to play a game or do a job.
We need helmets and other **equipment** to play football.

exclaimed   If someone **exclaimed** something, it was said in an excited way.
"Hooray!" the team **exclaimed** when they won.

excuse   If you say "**excuse** me," it is a polite way to get someone's attention.
She said "**excuse** me" before she asked us a question.

exercise   When you **exercise**, you move your body to get strong and healthy.
We **exercise** when we ride our bikes.

exercise

F

fan   If you are a **fan** of something, you like it very much.
I cheer for the team since I am a big **fan**.

fruits   The **fruits** of something are the good things that come from it.
The **fruits** of trying hard are learning new things and feeling proud.

fan

G

goal   When you get a **goal** in a game, you get one or more points.
I scored one **goal** in the game.

guy

guy A **guy** is a man or boy.

A **guy** named Joe drives the school bus.

H

heap A **heap** is a lot of something.

I have a **heap** of work to do today.

herd When you **herd** animals, you make them move together into a group.

They **herd** the sheep into the barn.

hero A **hero** is a person who does something brave to help others.

The man who saved the boy is a **hero**.

hero

honest   If you are an **honest** person, you tell the truth.
She was **honest** and told her mom she broke the cup.

honest

M

mammal   A **mammal** is a kind of animal that has hair and feeds milk to its babies.
A whale is a **mammal**, and so are cats and people.

O

once   If you do something **once** another thing happens, you do it right after.
I will do my homework **once** I finish eating.

mammal

227

P

predators Predators are animals that hunt other animals for food.
Little fish swim away from **predators** that want to eat them.

predators

prey An animal that is hunted by other animals is the **prey**.
Fish are a bear's **prey**.

prey

R

rules Rules tell what you can and cannot do.
We follow the **rules** when we play tag.

S

school   A big group of fish that swims together is called a **school**.
A big **school** of fish swam by our boat.

seed   A **seed** is a small, hard part of a plant that grows into a new plant.
A flower grew from the **seed** I planted in the dirt.

shingle   A **shingle** is a small, flat piece of wood, or something else, used to cover a roof.
A big wind blew a **shingle** off our roof.

short   A **short** time is a small amount of time.
We only waited a **short** time for the bus to come.

school

seed

shriek A **shriek** is a short, loud sound.
I made a loud **shriek** when I saw a snake.

soon If something will happen **soon**, it will happen a short time from now.
School is over, so we will be home **soon**.

sport A good **sport** plays fair and gets along with others.
He is a good **sport** and has fun even if he loses.

sport

stroll When you take a **stroll**, you go on a slow walk.
We took a **stroll** through the park.

surprise A **surprise** is something you did not know you would see or do.
The pet that Mom and Dad gave us was a big **surprise**!

surprise

T

team   A **team** is a group of people who play a game against another group.
Our **team** won the game today!

thank   You **thank** people when they do something nice for you.
I will **thank** him for the gift he gave me.

trouble   **Trouble** is a problem or something that is hard to fix.
We had **trouble** finding our lost dog.

twigs   **Twigs** are small, thin branches from a tree or bush.
The bird will build its nest with **twigs** from the tree.

team

twigs

231

W

warm

well

warm   If something is **warm**, it is a little bit hot.
I feel **warm** when I wear my hat and coat.

well   If you are **well**, you are healthy.
I feel **well** after I go for a long walk.

Index of Titles and Authors

Acknowledgments

A Big Guy Took My Ball! by Mo Willems. Copyright © 2013 by Mo Willems. Reprinted by permission of Disney Publishing Worldwide and Wernick & Pratt Agency.

Have You Heard the Nesting Bird? by Rita Gray, illustrated by Kenard Pak. Text copyright © 2014 by Rita Gray. Illustration copyright © 2014 by Kenard Pak. Reprinted by permission of Houghton Mifflin Harcourt Publishing Company.

"How to Defend Yourself Like an Armadillo," "How to Spin a Web Like a Spider," and "How to Trap Fish Like a Humpback Whale" from *How to Swallow a Pig* by Steve Jenkins and Robin Page. Copyright © 2015 by Houghton Mifflin Harcourt. Reprinted by permission of Houghton Mifflin Harcourt Publishing Company.

If You Plant a Seed by Kadir Nelson. Copyright © 2015 by Kadir Nelson. Reprinted by permission of HarperCollins Publishers.

Credits

4 (tl) ©flammulated/iStock/Getty Images Plus/Getty Images, (bl) ©Guenter Fischer/Getty Images, (br) ©Flickr/Ewen Charlton/Getty Images, (tr) ©Karel Gallas/Shutterstock; 5 (b) ©UbjsP/Shutterstock; 5 (tr) ©Flickr/Ewen Charlton/Getty Images; 6 (tl) (bg) ©Willard/iStock/Getty Images Plus/Getty Images, (inset) ©FatCamera/iStock/Getty Images Plus/Getty Images; 6 (bl) ©Blackout Concepts/Alamy; 7 (bl) (all) ©Better Worldians Foundation; 8 ©Sharon Haeger/Shutterstock; 9 ©StanislavBeloglazov/Shutterstock; 12 (bl) ©MikeCardUK/iStock/Getty Images Plus/Getty Images; 12 (br) ©Sean Wandzilak/Shutterstock; 13 (bl) ©Remsberg Inc./Design Pics/Getty Images; 13 (br) ©cowboy5437/iStock/Getty Images Plus/Getty Images; 14 ©Jim Ruther Nill; 38 ©James Bruchac; 56 Courtesy of Houghton Mifflin Harcourt; 78 (tr) ©Neirfy/Shutterstock; 78 (tr) ©Yulia_Malinovskaya/iStock/Getty Images Plus; 78 (bg) ©aboutsung/Shutterstock; 79 ©Brian Kushner/Alamy; 80 ©wwing/iStock/Getty Images Plus/Getty Images; 82 Courtesy of Houghton Mifflin Harcourt; 100 (inset) ©Chase Dekker Wild-Life Images/Getty Images; 100 (bg) ©UbjsP/Shutterstock; 101 (inset) ©All For You/Shutterstock; 102 ©National Geographic Stock; 103 (tr) ©UbjsP/Shutterstock; 104 ©Bertrand Demee/Photographer's Choice/Getty Images; 105 ©Holly Kuchera/Shutterstock; 106 (br) ©Patricia Doyle/Photographer's Choice/Getty Images, (cl) ©Be Good/Shutterstock, (bcr) ©MidoSemsem/Shutterstock, (cr) ©Lane Oatey/Blue Jean Images/Getty Images, (l) ©ImagesBazaar/Getty Images, (c) ©Dmytro Zinkevych/Shutterstock, (bg) ©Bimbim/Shutterstock; 110 (bg) ©Willard/iStock/Getty Images Plus/Getty Images, (inset) ©FatCamera/iStock/Getty Images Plus/Getty Images; 111 (tl) ©GagliardiImages/Shutterstock; 111 (tr) ©Blend Images/Alamy Images; 111 (br) ©Houghton Mifflin Harcourt; 112 ©Jane Medina; 114 ©AP/Houghton Mifflin Harcourt; 126 ©AP/Houghton Mifflin Harcourt; 130 (t) ©Kanan Shabanov/Shutterstock; 131 (tl) ©Andersen Ross/Media Bakery; 131 (tr) ©Mladen Mitrinovic/Shutterstock; 132 ©Kiankhoon/iStock/Getty Images Plus/Getty Images; 134 ©Cristian Mallery Williams; 135 ©Blackout Concepts/Alamy; 136 (b) ©FatCamera/iStock/Getty Images Plus; 136 (inset) ©Ivan Nikulin/Shutterstock; 137 (c) ©Sonya Etchison/Shutterstock; 137 (inset) ©Ivan Nikulin/Shutterstock; 138 (b) ©Monkey Business Images/iStock/Getty Images Plus/Getty Images; 138 (inset) ©Ivan Nikulin/Shutterstock; 139 (c) ©Monkey Business Images/Getty Images; 139 (inset) ©Ivan Nikulin/Shutterstock; 140 (b) ©Getty Images; 140 (inset) ©Ivan Nikulin/Shutterstock; 141 (r) ©DenKuvaiev/iStockPhoto.com; 141 (inset) ©Ivan Nikulin/Shutterstock; 142 (c) ©Getty Images; 142 (inset) ©Ivan Nikulin/Shutterstock; 143 (b) ©FatCamera/iStock/Getty Images Plus/Getty Images; 143 (inset) ©Ivan Nikulin/Shutterstock; 144 (tc) ©Jim Erickson/Media Bakery; 144 (tl) ©Don Mason/Getty Images; 144 (tr) ©SHOTFILE/Alamy Images; 144 (bl) ©DoublePHOTO studio/Shutterstock; 144 (bc) ©warrengoldswain/iStock/Getty Images Plus/Getty Images; 144 (br) ©fakezzz/iStock/Getty Images Plus/Getty Images; 144 (cr) ©Blend Images/Alamy; 144 (c) ©JHershPhotography/iStock/Getty Images; 144 (cl) ©bradleym/iStock/Getty Images Plus/Getty Images; 144 (inset) ©Ivan Nikulin/Shutterstock; 144 (inset) ©Ivan Nikulin/Shutterstock; 144 (inset) ©Ivan Nikulin/Shutterstock; 145 (tr) ©Blackout Concepts/Alamy; 147 (tr) ©Blackout Concepts/Alamy; 148 (bg) ©denisik11/iStock/Getty Images Plus/Getty Images; 148 (t) ©iStock/Getty Images Plus/Getty Images; 148 (cl) ©Rawpixel/iStock/Getty Images Plus/Getty Images; 148 (tl) ©shapecharge/iStock/Getty Images Plus/Getty Images; 149 (c) ©Houghton Mifflin Harcourt; 149 (r) ©Houghton Mifflin Harcourt; 150 (tr) ©Rawpixel/iStock/Getty Images Plus/Getty Images; 150 (tl) ©shapecharge/iStock/Getty Images Plus/Getty Images; 150 (tl) ©denisik11/iStock/Getty Images Plus/Getty Images; 216 ©Weekend Images Inc./Getty Images; 217 (all) ©Better Worldians Foundation; 218 ©Better Worldians Foundation; 220 ©FatCamera/iStock/Getty Images Plus/Getty Images; 221 ©Dragon Images/Shutterstock; 222 (t) ©Rubberball/Getty Images; 222 (b) ©Jason Gallier/Alamy; 223 (b) ©Edgar Bullon/Shutterstock; 223 (t) ©Houghton Mifflin Harcourt; 224 (t) ©Moment Open/Getty Images; 224 (b) ©Comstock/Getty Images; 225 (b) ©ESB Professional/Shutterstock; 225 (t) ©Monkey Business Images/Shutterstock; 226 (t) ©bikeriderlondon/Shutterstock; 226 (b) ©SanchalRat/Shutterstock; 227 (b) ©Yann Hubert/Shutterstock; 227 (t) ©Alfira/Shutterstock; 228 (t) ©CatPix-The Art of Nature/Moment/Getty Images; 228 (b) ©giv58/Fotolia; 229 (t) ©Getty Images; 229 (b) ©Houghton Mifflin Harcourt; 230 (b) ©vectorfusionart/Shutterstock; 230 (t) ©YakobchukOlena/Shutterstock; 231 (b) ©William Leaman/Alamy; 231 (t) ©Lucky Business/Shutterstock; 232 (t) ©LWA/Dann Tardif/Getty Images; 232 (b) ©Houghton Mifflin Harcourt